Essential Question
Why do people run for public office?

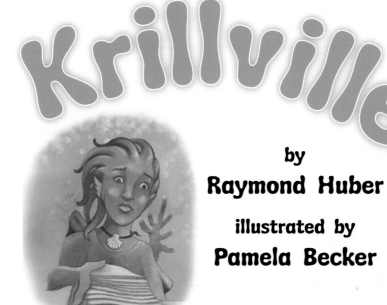

by
Raymond Huber

illustrated by
Pamela Becker

Chapter 1
Kelp! 2

Chapter 2
The Petition.................................6

Chapter 3
Rules 11

Respond to Reading.........................16

PAIRED READ Running a Town 17

Focus on Literary Elements..................20

Chapter 1 | Kelp!

It all started with kelp. I was on my way home when I saw some young aqualings playing in the kelp forest. They were having great fun whooshing down the wide, slippery kelp blades. Krillville is a small village, and the kelp is the only good play area we have. As I was swimming away, I heard a shout.

"Hey! Go home, you naughty aqualings." It was Mr. Crab, one of the town's council members, yelling at another group of children playing hide-and-seek among the kelp fronds. I knew Mr. Crab's bark was worse than his bite, so I swam over to talk to him.

"Good morning, Mr. Crab. Is everything okay?"

"No, it's not, Maribel. These young aqualings need to stop clowning around and go home."

"Kids will be kids, Mr. C. Are they too noisy?"

He shook his head and clicked his tongue. "No, no. I can tolerate their noise. They need to go home because we're closing the forest. We're going to clear-cut the kelp."

I was so shocked that I could barely speak. "Excuse me, but did you say 'clear-cut the kelp'?"

"Yes, Maribel, all this kelp will be chopped down to the seabed."

"But you can't do that, Mr. Crab," I spluttered. "It's against the law!"

"Nonsense. A majority of the council has voted for this project, and everything's being done according to village planning procedures."

"What project?" I asked.

"An impressive new housing development. The largest giant-clam houses you've ever seen, plus a landfood restaurant. It will bring a much-needed touch of class to Krillville."

"But the kelp forest is the only area for young aqualings in Krillville to play," I replied.

"Nonsense. They will still have the whale skeleton!"

I pictured the old rib cage that sat in the village square. "True, but it's so small. There's not enough room for all the children to play there."

Mr. Crab clicked his tongue loudly. "It's too late for debates, Maribel. The council intends to go ahead with this development for the good of all aqualings. Besides, it's been done according to the rules."

I went home wondering how I could save the kelp from destruction. Mr. Crab's words rolled around in my mind: "It's been done according to the rules." Maybe there were some other rules that I could use to make the council change its mind. I decided to talk to the aqualing who led the Krillville council: Mayor Mudskipper.

The next morning, I swam to the council caves. It was a slow trip against a cool current that was flowing through the village. I discovered the mayor in his office.

"Good morning, Maribel," he said from behind a towering stack of papers. "Please excuse the mess. Now, how can I help?"

I told the mayor how upset I was to hear from Mr. Crab that the kelp was going to be cut down.

"Yes, you're right," he said. "I never realized the young aqualings played there, but the new clam houses will be magnificent."

"Is there any way of persuading the council to change its mind?" I asked.

"Let me see," Mayor Mudskipper replied. He rustled around in his papers and gurgled to himself. "Ah, here it is," he said. "There's a rule that says if a majority of aqualings in Krillville sign a petition against a council decision, the council must take another vote."

This was just the kind of news I had been hoping for!

"So I need to collect signatures from everyone who wants to save the kelp forest?"

"You can try, Maribel, but don't count your tadpoles before they hatch—not everyone will agree with you."

Despite the mayor's words of caution, I left his cave confident that most residents would support my campaign to keep the kelp.

Chapter 2 | The Petition

When I arrived home, I got my bottle of octopus ink and carefully wrote a petition in my neatest handwriting. Then I visited our neighbors, a family of five who lived in the next clam shell. Mrs. Anchovy came to the door.

"Hello, Maribel."

"Hi, Mrs. Anchovy. Would you like to sign my petition? I'm trying to save the kelp forest as a play area for children."

She read the petition. "Yes, I'll sign it all right. I took my kids to play there this morning, but it was closed off. They were so disappointed." She scrawled her name on the petition.

"Thank you so much," I said.

"I'm just glad someone is standing up for young aqualings," Mrs. Anchovy replied.

My first signature! It was a drop in the ocean, but it was a beginning. Encouraged by Mrs. Anchovy, I went from shell to shell along the entire street.

Most of my neighbors agreed with the petition, and the school principal, Ms. Minnow, even circulated a copy among the teachers. The Fin twins, Blue and Dolph, helped me knock on doors for the rest of the afternoon.

I was surprised to find, however, that not everyone agreed with my petition. Some, such as Mr. and Mrs. Hammerhead, liked the idea of fancy clam mansions and did not care about the kelp. "We can rename our village Bubberly Hills!" Mrs. Hammerhead exclaimed.

I managed to visit most of the Krillville residents, and I arrived home just as the tide was going out. I was weary but satisfied with the petition, which already had ten pages of signatures. Many aqualing parents had signed because they wanted to save the kelp for their children, and most aqualings believed the kelp was important for the environment, too.

I nervously counted the signatures to see if I had a majority. Yes! More than half the villagers had signed my petition. I would present it at the council meeting tomorrow, and then the kelp forest would be saved. I went to sleep that night feeling very pleased with my day's work.

The next morning, I arrived early at the town hall to make sure my petition would be discussed at the meeting. The council members were gathering outside, and I spotted Mayor Mudskipper as he was about to enter the hall.

"I did it, Mr. Mayor—I got the support of a majority of villagers!" I exclaimed as I handed him the petition.

"Oh, dear me, Maribel, that's wonderful work, but ..."

"But what? Is there something wrong?"

"Look," said Mayor Mudskipper, pointing into the meeting room. Mr. Crab floated in the middle of a circle of council members. It was obvious that he was talking to them forcefully. The water bubbled as he swished his claws around him for emphasis.

"You have an opponent, Maribel. I'm afraid Mr. Crab heard about your petition, and he's trying to turn the undecided council members against it."

I was not allowed into the meeting room once the meeting had started, so I sat outside and waited. Would they accept my petition and vote to stop the project? Or would they listen to Mr. Crab's opinion and decide to go ahead and cut down the kelp?

At last the meeting was over, and the council members drifted out and swam past me. Mayor Mudskipper came and sat beside me.

"Sorry, Maribel. I voted for you, but the petition was narrowly defeated. The kelp cutting is going ahead."

This was such a surprise that it took a moment for the news to sink in—I had lost! "But surely there must be something else I can do to stop it?" I pleaded.

"We'll try to think of an alternative," the mayor replied. "Perhaps we can find a larger play-skeleton for the village square."

Just then, Mr. Crab came out of the meeting room looking very proud with his head held high.

"It was an extremely close vote, Maribel," he announced, "but rules are rules. Now, I can't dawdle. I'm going home to watch the National Bubbleball Finals on Ocean TV." Mr. Crab hurriedly swam off.

"I must go, too, Maribel," the mayor said. "The governor is visiting tomorrow, and I'd better tidy up my office beforehand."

He dashed away, leaving me all alone and feeling desperate. Despite so many signatures on my petition, I was back to square one. I tried to recover my resolve— there had to be another solution. I decided to swim home past the kelp. Maybe I would get some inspiration by looking at the precious play area.

As the expanse of kelp came into view, a terrible sight met my eyes.

A group of workers was attacking the kelp with shell-saws, the sharp blades whacking through the seaweed as if it was jelly. Chomp! Splat! Soon there would be nothing left but seabed.

I rushed forward, but a worker held me back.

"Hold your seahorses!" he yelled. "You'll get squashed."

"You have to stop!" I yelled back. "Just think of all the children—they love the kelp forest!"

"That is not my problem. Now stand back, please. I have to finish this job before the bubbleball game starts."

I couldn't bear to watch the destruction, so I swam home. It was so overwhelming that I felt like giving up.

I went to bed with three words swirling around in my brain: "Rules are rules..."

Chapter 3 | Rules

I woke early the next day. The tide was just beginning to go out again, and I could hear whales singing in the distance. In the middle of the night, I'd had an idea. I put on my best clothes and swam down to the town hall. I felt a change in the water, and a warm current carried me quickly into the village square.

As I had anticipated, the governor of Aqualina had just arrived with his entourage, and I knew that this was my last chance. His muscled bodyguard glared at me fiercely, but nothing was going to put me off.

"Excuse me, Governor!" I called as the guard quickly moved between us and loomed over me.

"It's okay, Ray," the governor said, and the guard stepped aside. "Ray accompanies me everywhere—he's just doing his job."

"I need your advice, Governor," I said. "It's urgent."

"What's the problem?" he asked.

I told the governor all about the clam housing project, the kelp cutting, and the rejection of my petition.

I asked him if there was anything he could do for the children of Krillville. The governor reached into his briefcase and pulled out an enormous book.

"This is the Constitution of the State of Aquilina," he said. "It contains all the rules for our state. Take it home and study it. You might find the answer you're looking for."

I took the book home and began to read the constitution. The print was almost microscopic, and the words were hard to understand. I looked up "playground" in the index, but there was nothing listed. Then I realized they probably used big words in government, so I looked again, and sure enough, there was a section called "Recreation for Youth." I held my breath as I read:

> **Village councils must provide aqualing youth with adequate recreation and sporting facilities free of charge.**

This was the rule that I had been hoping for all along.

Maybe it was too late to save the kelp, but now I had a new strategy in mind. First, I would go and visit Mr. Crab; he was the one I needed to convince most of all.

When I arrived at Mr. Crab's, I opened the book and turned to the rule about recreation for aqualing youth.

"Krillville has no area for sports," I pointed out politely.

Mr. Crab clicked his tongue. "I hate to admit it, but you're right, Maribel. It says that the council must support sports for youth. It's a state law."

"Rules are rules," I replied. Mr. Crab had to smile at that!

"But where will we find the space?" he asked.

"We already have the space where the kelp forest used to be," I said. "We just need to share it." I explained my idea, and Mr. Crab's smile broadened.

It took months to put my plan into action, but the council worked hard, and eventually it was completed. The whole of Krillville turned out for the grand opening of the new Bubberly Park. On one side, there was a double stack of tidy clam shells—not huge mansions but comfortable apartments. On the other half of the park was a beautiful bubbleball court with bleachers around it.

Mayor Mudskipper stood up to make his speech. He began, "Aqualings of Krillville, I now declare Bubberly Park officially open!"

Applause rippled through the crowd, and the mayor continued, "We now have a wonderful bubbleball court for our children to play on, and as a bonus, the residents of the new Clammy Apartments also have great views of the games. This is all thanks to Maribel's determination. She reminded us that the rules should work for the benefit of all. A big cheer for Maribel!"

The applause sent waves through the park. The sound of all those excited aqualings made me feel like it had been worth the effort.

During the months of planning and building, I had noticed other things that we needed to do in the village: plant a new kelp forest, buy more sea-books for the library, and provide shells for the homeless hermits. I knew now that change was possible, and I was determined to run for a seat on the council once I was old enough. Who knows, one day I might even make it to the Governor's Mansion in Sploshington.

But for now, I settled back in my comfortable seat to watch the opening game of the bubbleball season, the Slicks versus the Wets.

Respond to Reading

Summarize

Use important details from *Krillville* to summarize the story. Your graphic organizer may help.

Details

↓

Author's Point of View

Text Evidence

1. How do you know that this story is a fantasy?
   GENRE

2. From what point of view is this story told? Give details from the text that show who the narrator is.
   POINT OF VIEW

3. What does "Mr. Crab's bark was worse than his bite" mean on page 2? **IDIOMS**

4. Write about how this story would be different if it were told by a third-person narrator. **WRITE ABOUT READING**

Compare Texts
Read about what a town council does.

Running a Town

The people who live in towns and cities require all kinds of services, such as public transportation, schools, libraries, drinking water, and playgrounds. The town or city council is responsible for organizing these services.

Electing the Town or City Council

The members of a town or city council are elected by the residents of the city or town. The town council in a small town might have between 5 and 10 members. City councils in bigger cities might have 50 members. Elections are usually held every two or four years. In larger towns and cities, the residents also elect a mayor.

A person on a town council is said to hold public office. People who run for public office care about their communities and want to make their communities better places to live.

A candidate meets voters before an election.

17

Making Decisions

City and town councils have regular meetings to discuss local issues, to decide how to spend the money in the budget, and to plan for the future of the community. City and town councils also make new rules to protect people in the community or to improve life in a community.

Town and city council meetings are often open to the public, and records of the meetings are also available. Residents are able to find out what the members of a city or town council are working on. In addition, the town's residents can go to meetings or approach their council member with ideas or problems. For example, a neighborhood group might present a petition for a new bike path. People can report problems, such as graffiti or a broken streetlight. Council members discuss important issues and then vote on them.

Town councils also work with the state government to meet the needs of local areas.

THE STATE CONSTITUTION

The United States is so big that each state has its own government. States also have state constitutions, which protect the rights of their citizens. State governments and town or city councils work together to help things run smoothly.

Providing Services

Every town has roads to repair, trash to collect, and libraries to run. The council employs many people to do these jobs. The council pays for these services with money received from taxes that are paid by people who own property in the town.

The council has committees, or small groups, that make decisions about the different services, such as libraries or trash collection.

A town council works to make the town a better place to live and work in. Council members encourage people to bring their businesses to town, and they take care of the residents' needs.

These council members are meeting to discuss a local issue.

Make Connections

How does a town council help people?
ESSENTIAL QUESTION

What similarities are there between the council in *Krillville* and town councils in *Running a Town*?
TEXT TO TEXT

Focus on
Literary Elements

Onomatopoeia Onomatopoeia means a word that sounds like the thing it stands for. There are many examples of onomatopoeia in the words we use for animal sounds. *Woof, meow, croak,* and *cluck* all sound like the sounds made by different animals.

Read and Find On page 2 of *Krillville*, the word *whooshed* encourages you to draw out the "oosh" in the middle and make a long sound, like the sound an aqualing would make sliding down a slippery kelp blade.

On page 10, the words *whacking, chomp,* and *splat* help us to "hear" the sounds of the kelp being chopped down.

Your Turn

Write a group soundscape using onomatopoeia. Make a T-chart with the heading "Setting" for one column and "Sounds" for the other. Fill in the chart with at least four settings and two or three sounds for each. On your own, choose one setting and write a paragraph using as much onomatopoeia as possible.

Read your paragraph aloud to your group or your class and adjust it to form a soundscape that you can illustrate and share with others.